D0710297

ESCAPE
AND EVASION

ELITE FORCES SURVIVAL GUIDE SERIES

Elite Survival
Survive in the Desert with the French Foreign Legion
Survive in the Arctic with the Royal Marine Commandos
Survive in the Mountains with the U.S. Rangers and Army
   Mountain Division
Survive in the Jungle with the Special Forces "Green Berets"
Survive in the Wilderness with the Canadian and Australian
   Special Forces
Survive at Sea with the U.S. Navy SEALs
Training to Fight with the Parachute Regiment
The World's Best Soldiers

Elite Operations and Training
Escape and Evasion
Surviving Captivity with the U.S. Air Force
Hostage Rescue with the SAS
How to Pass Elite Forces Selection
Learning Mental Endurance with the U.S. Marines

Special Forces Survival Guidebooks
Survival Equipment
Navigation and Signaling
Surviving Natural Disasters
Using Ropes and Knots
Survival First Aid
Trapping, Fishing, and Plant Food
Urban Survival Techniques

ESCAPE
AND EVASION

CHRIS McNAB

Introduction by Colonel John T. Carney. Jr., USAF–Ret.
President, Special Operations Warrior Foundation

MASON CREST PUBLISHERS

This edition first published in 2003
by Mason Crest Publishers Inc.
370 Reed Road, Broomall, PA, 19008

Library of Congress Cataloging-in-Publication Data available

ISBN 1-59084-009-7

Editorial and design by
Amber Books Ltd.
Bradley's Close
74–77 White Lion Street
London N1 9PF

Project Editor Chris Stone
Designer Simon Thompson
Picture Research Lisa Wren

Printed and bound in Malaysia

10 9 8 7 6 5 4 3 2 1

ACKNOWLEDGMENT
For authenticating this book, the Publishers would like to thank the Public Affairs Offices of the U.S. Special Operations Command, MacDill AFB, FL.; Army Special Operations Command, Fort Bragg, N.C.; Navy Special Warfare Command, Coronado, CA.; and the Air Force Special Operations Command, Hurlbert Field, FL.

IMPORTANT NOTICE
The survival techniques and information described in this publication are for use in dire circumstances where the safety of the individual is at risk. Accordingly, the publisher cannot accept any responsibility for any prosecution or proceedings brought or instituted against any person or body as a result of the uses or misuses of the techniques and information within.

DEDICATION
This book is dedicated to those who perished in the terrorist attacks of September 11, 2001, and to the Special Forces soldiers who continually serve to defend freedom.

Picture Credits
Corbis: 6, 10, 13, 20, 28, 29, 32, 34, 36, 42, 45, 50, 53; **Military Picture Library**: 48; **TRH**: 8, 16, 37, 40, 44, 54; **US Dept. of Defense**: 18, 22, 24, 27, 58.
lllustrations courtesy of Amber Books and De Agostini UK and the following supplied by Patrick Mulrey: 14.
Front cover: **Corbis** (inset), **TRH** (main)

CONTENTS

INTRODUCTION

Elite forces are the tip of Freedom's spear. These small, special units are universally the first to engage, whether on reconnaissance missions into denied territory for larger, conventional forces or in direct action, surgical operations, preemptive strikes, retaliatory action, and hostage rescues. They lead the way in today's war on terrorism, the war on drugs, the war on transnational unrest, and in humanitarian operations as well as nation building. When large scale warfare erupts, they offer theater commanders a wide variety of unique, unconventional options.

Most such units are regionally oriented, acclimated to the culture and conversant in the languages of the areas where they operate. Since they deploy to those areas regularly, often for combined training exercises with indigenous forces, these elite units also serve as peacetime "global scouts" and "diplomacy multipliers," a beacon of hope for the democratic aspirations of oppressed peoples all over the globe.

Elite forces are truly "quiet professionals": their actions speak louder than words. They are self-motivated, self-confident, versatile, seasoned, mature individuals who rely on teamwork more than daring-do. Unfortunately, theirs is dangerous work. Since "Desert One"—the 1980 attempt to rescue hostages from the U.S. embassy in Tehran, for instance—American special operations forces have suffered casualties in real world operations at close to fifteen times the rate of U.S. conventional forces. By the very nature of the challenges which face special operations forces, training for these elite units has proven even more hazardous.

Thus it's with special pride that I join you in saluting the brave men and women who volunteer to serve in and support these magnificent units and who face such difficult challenges ahead.

Colonel John T. Carney, Jr., USAF–Ret.
President, Special Operations Warrior Foundation

In the 1980s, U.S. Navy SEALs used their advanced escape and evasion tactics to assist the military forces in El Salvador and Honduras.

WORKING BEHIND ENEMY LINES

The soldiers who survive and fight behind enemy lines have to be the best in the world. For weeks at a time, they must be vigilant every second of the day, for a mistake can be fatal.

There are many reasons why soldiers go undercover behind enemy lines. Sometimes they need to observe what the enemy is doing and report back to headquarters. Other times they actually go there to fight, destroying enemy bases or equipment. On other occasions, they go there to rescue prisoners. Because of their expertise, elite soldiers rarely participate in standard warfare. Since World War II, Special Forces have engaged in all manner of Unconventional Warfare including sabotage, and going undercover to fight terrorists and **guerrilla** soldiers (known as "**counterinsurgency**").

All these operations need a special breed of soldier. Undercover operations are fought by soldiers who can actually put themselves into a foreign society and either stay hidden or blend into the background so that they are not noticed. In this book, we will reveal the exceptional skills and qualities of an undercover warrior. Surviving behind enemy lines demands great intelligence, creative thinking, and self-control. Those who go on these missions are some of the world's most talented military minds.

Soldiers must stay close to the ground to keep out of sight. This technique, known as "eating dirt," is common to all special forces.

First, let's look at what sort of person you need to be to work as an undercover or counterinsurgency soldier. The U.S. Army has many different tests to determine who is suited to this dangerous work. They have devised a list of seven different characteristics that undercover soldiers must have. They must be resistant to mental and physical tiredness. They must be able to solve difficult

This member of the Venezualan Special Forces is taught counter-insurgency tactics by U.S. Green Berets in the Orinoco jungle. It is important he keeps his M16 rifle dry at all times.

problems. They must be able to work as part of a team. They must face danger with resolution, courage, and intelligence. They must have the ability to remember military information. They must show a willingness to work hard in training and never give up. They must be able to cope with being isolated and working on their own.

If the recruiters can find someone with these qualities, then that person can qualify to be an undercover elite soldier. Such a soldier must acquire an amazing variety of combat, survival, and tactical skills. These include:

• Using weapons, including rifles, machine guns, explosives, and methods of destroying enemy tanks and aircraft.
• Never getting lost during navigation across difficult terrain.
• **Tracking** the enemy over long distances without being seen.
• Communicating using modern radios and technology.
• Directing artillery fire and air strikes precisely at their targets.
• Setting and detecting mines and **booby traps**.
• Mountaineering.
• First aid.
• Sailing and diving.

Since the list of skills is very long, it can take many years to train a specialist soldier such as a Special Air Service (SAS) fighter, Special Forces, or a U.S. Navy SEAL.

But the role of the undercover soldier is not just about fighting and combat. Special forces soldiers often have to go into foreign villages and towns, and make friends with the local people. This is so the soldier can either find out more information about the enemy, or get people to trust them so that the civilians themselves

In Vietnam, U.S. Special Forces became experts in jungle camouflage, working in detachments of 10 to 12 men. They trained the South Vietnamese in basic field craft.

will help fight the enemy. A good example of this was the U.S. Fifth Special Forces group (5SPG) in the Vietnam War. Part of their job was to create what were called **Civilian Irregular Defense Groups** (CIDGs). These were essentially bands of Vietnamese civilians persuaded by the U.S. troops to fight on their side against the communists. By making friends with the people, the Special Forces enlisted around 42,000 CIDG soldiers.

We can now see that it takes more than combat skills to be a successful undercover soldier. There are several other essential skills. An ability to learn new languages is one of them. Soldiers should be able to speak in the foreign language without stumbling over their words—if they cannot speak it fluently, then they will give themselves away during the operation. They should also be good at negotiating with people. This does not mean always getting their own way. Instead it means that soldiers truly listen to other people and try to find solutions to problems that make everyone happy. If they can do this, then they are more likely to persuade others to be on their side because others will trust them. Undercover soldiers must also be able to impersonate people if they

Sniping requires an effective use of camouflage. This U.S. soldier uses an optical sight to magnify his target and bring it within range.

are to blend in with foreign peoples when on operations. They must observe the way people dress, speak, act, and think, and be able to imitate these characteristics. If they cannot, then they will stand out and most likely be discovered by the enemy soldiers.

There is one other quality that undercover soldiers must have—they must be able to keep a secret. Some people want to be undercover soldiers in order to brag about it. These people are

When working behind enemy lines, a special forces soldier must dress as a civilian to avoid detection. In this situation, the soldier uses a plain-looking sack to conceal his change of clothes and equipment.

never accepted into the job. Because elite soldiers deal with such important missions, they are trusted with very secret information. If they boast about their work to parents, spouses, and friends, they can put other people's lives in danger. That is why an undercover soldier must be able to have a secret and never tell a single person about it (apart from those people to whom he or she is meant to talk). Soldiers often need to hold these secrets for the rest of their lives.

Now we see what exceptional people undercover soldiers are. What we will turn to next is how they actually get behind enemy lines in the first place. This is known as **"infiltration."**

OBSERVATION SKILLS

Observation is one of the most important skills for undercovers soldiers, who must be alert at all times. This means that they use all their senses to take in as much information from the world around them. Nothing must be missed. The soldier must be aware of colors, shapes, movements, noises, odors, and sensations. Anything could provide a vital clue about danger approaching. In the Vietnam War, for example, trampled grass, signs of garbage, or even a single twig out of place by the side of a road might have indicated to a U.S. patrol that there was a booby trap or ambush waiting for them. By reading these warnings, troops can stay one step ahead of the enemy.

INFILTRATION BY AIR

Infiltration means getting into enemy territory without being discovered. This is not easy when the enemy is watching and waiting. That is why using parachutes or aircraft are one of the quickest methods.

Most elite units train their soldiers in parachute techniques. At the very least, this means training the soldiers to do what are known as "**static-line drops**." Here, a large number of troops jump from a transport aircraft and their parachutes open automatically. Yet this method is slow and the transport aircraft are vulnerable to being shot down. That is why some new methods of parachuting have been designed.

A swifter and more secret way of putting soldiers behind enemy lines from the air is called High-Altitude, Low-Opening (**HALO**) parachuting. In this case, the troops jump from the aircraft at an altitude of some 32,000 feet (10,000 m). They do not open their parachutes immediately. Instead, they freefall to an altitude of about 2,500 feet (760 m), and then they open their parachutes. This means that they get from the aircraft to the ground very quickly, and are less likely to be spotted by the enemy.

However, HALO parachuting requires a lot of training. The freefaller, for example, has to keep a stable position during the flight wearing a heavy backpack and a weapon strapped to the body

U.S. Airborne Forces make a rapid rope descent from a Black Hawk helicopter during Operation "Desert Storm" in 1991.

A U.S. Army parachute team make a jump during the Australian "Tandem Thrust" exercise in 1997. The team must all jump within one minute, in order to stay together when behind enemy lines.

by a harness. At high altitudes, the HALO jumpers also need oxygen-breathing equipment—there is not enough air to breathe at 10,000 feet (3,100 m). They are falling so fast they need a special machine called a "**barometric trigger**" to open their parachutes automatically at the right altitude. If they leave it until too late, they could hit the ground before their parachutes open properly.

In addition, the paratroopers will be exposed to freezing temperatures as they freefall. This may result in ice forming on their equipment, especially their goggles. These problems mean that HALO jumpers need to be in prime physical shape and highly

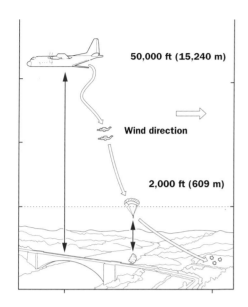

HALO tactics requires troops to open parachutes relatively late.

skilled, both of which require a great deal of time and training. As a result, only the best elite units train their soldiers in HALO parachuting techniques, such as the SAS units and the U.S. Navy SEALs.

HAHO parachuting is different from HALO parachuting. This stands for High-Altitude, High-Opening. Again paratroopers are dropped from the aircraft wearing oxygen-breathing equipment at an altitude of 32,000 feet (10,000 m). However, they freefall for only 8 to 10 seconds, then open the parachute at around 27,600 feet (8,500 m). They then slowly, silently, float to the ground. This can take between 70 and 80 minutes, by which time they will have traveled up to 19 miles (30 km). This means the team can be dropped outside enemy territory, and then drift behind enemy lines unseen by radar. But there are problems with HAHO parachuting. The team must stay together once the parachutes are opened to be sure

HAHO parachuting requires the soldier to "fly" down.

Freefall parachuting feels like floating on a cushion of air. Yet these U.S. Airborne soldiers are actually falling at around 160 miles per hour (250 km/h) and must be ready to pull their ripcord in time to land safely.

of landing together. This can be very difficult, because winds can scatter people for miles. All the soldiers must be experts at "flying" their parachutes if they are to land together.

A way around the problem of parachuting elite teams is to land aircraft on runways and simply offload the occupants. During World War II, for example, British SAS teams in France after **D-Day** sometimes made use of the single-engined Lysander aircraft to evacuate wounded personnel, agents, or downed Allied airmen. Aircraft such as the Lysander require an airstrip at least 300 feet (92 m) long, but heavier transports need runways at least 1,200 feet

LANDING BY HELICOPTER

When an elite forces unit lands by helicopter, it must follow this procedure:

- Get out of the helicopter as quickly as possible, keeping low to avoid the rotor blades spinning above their heads.
- Adopt defensive positions immediately on all sides of the helicopter—the noise of the helicopter will mean that they cannot hear gunfire if the enemy shooting at them.
- Spend two or three minutes after the helicopter has left getting used to the silence and environment. This means sitting still without talking, listening and watching carefully for signs of the approaching enemy.
- Work out exactly where the helicopter has dropped the unit before moving off.

(370 m) to land and take off safely. If an established runway is not available, a rough strip will have to be built. Ideally, elite teams arrive and leave during darkness, so the airstrip will need some sort of illumination to guide in the pilot.

Once on the ground, whether by parachute or leaving a landed aircraft, the leader will gather together the team. Each member of the team will have memorized the location or where they are meant to meet—called the "**Rendezvous Point.**" To assist in gathering the team, the commander will activate a portable radio homing beacon, which emits a weak, high-frequency signal. When the other team members land, they activate their personal handheld radio receivers, which pick up the commander's signals and convert them into a bleeping noise. The signal becomes stronger when the radio receiver is pointed directly at the beacon, which leads the team to the

U.S. Black Hawk helicopters in action during the Gulf War in 1991. Each helicopter can carry up to 11 Special Forces troops.

commander. Once the team is all together, all parachute equipment is buried. Nothing is left that might tell the enemy that a special forces team has landed.

Despite the parachute training given to elite troops, helicopters are now the most popular method of infiltration for specialist teams. The United States leads the way with regard to helicopter technology. The advantage of modern helicopters, such as the UH-60 Black Hawk, is that they can fly at treetop level, underneath enemy radar. This is dangerous flying, especially at night, and helicopters usually fly at a speed of no greater than 90 miles per hour (140 km/h). At such speeds, helicopters can be flown by pilots wearing night vision goggles, which let them see in the dark. Flying at such altitudes means running the risk of being hit by enemy ground fire, especially from troops.

Once the helicopter arrives at its destination—known as the **"Drop Zone"** (DZ)—the team must get out as quickly as possible. This means throwing packs out of the doors and jumping out with guns, prepared for action in case the enemy are waiting for them. Normally the helicopter will touch down, but in long grass or uneven terrain it will hover at around six feet (1.8 m), which means the soldiers will have to jump to the ground. When being picked up, the team should enter the aircraft in the reverse order that they left the aircraft. The team leader should then confirm that everyone is safely aboard before telling the pilot to take off.

Aircraft and parachute landings make fast methods of infiltration. But sometimes other methods are needed.

INFILTRATION BY SEA AND LAND

Infiltration across sea or land requires amazing concentration and nerves of steel. All noises must be kept to a minimum, otherwise the enemy will become alerted that an elite unit is in its midst.

Rivers and coastlines offer elite forces units another way of covertly infiltrating enemy territory. Waterborne operations require troops who are highly trained in the use of underwater breathing equipment. Teams using **scuba** equipment can infiltrate harbors and rivers, either to move farther inland or to carry out sabotage missions against shipping or coastal targets. To do so, elite units such as the U.S. Navy SEALs and British Special Boat Service (SBS) use specially designed oxygen tanks that do not let out clouds of bubbles when the soldier breathes out. This is because an enemy soldier on a ship might see the bubbles and know that there is a diver below. The special tanks also give the soldier about four hours of underwater breathing. Each diver will also have to carry his or her equipment and explosives, including **limpet mines**. These are stuck to the side of ships and can weigh up to 33 pounds (17 kg). Because of the exertion involved in military diving, the maximum distance for a combat swim is around nine-tenths of a mile (1.5 km).

U.S. Marines favor the M16 gun. Behind enemy lines, this relatively light weapon (8 lb/3.7 kg) helps the soldier move swiftly to his target.

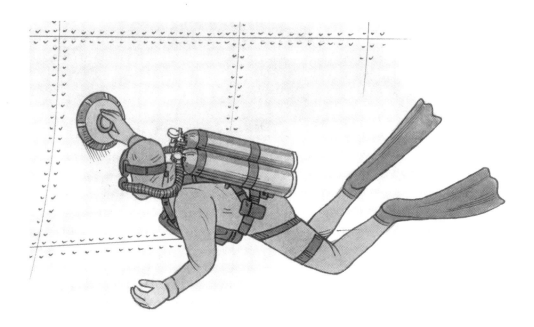

A U.S. Navy SEALs combat diver sticks a magnetic limpet mine to the side of a ship. On missions like this, the soldier will be equipped with exposure suit, fins, depth gauge, breathing apparatus, and compass.

Because of the problems of swimming to the target, many elite units use special floating vehicles to take teams to the target. A recent invention is the so-called subskimmer. This is a semi-inflatable "boat" that can travel on the surface and underwater. To turn it into a submarine is simple: the soldier seals off the engine and instrument compartment and then deflates the side tubes. The subskimmer can approach the target underwater, powered by two electric motors. And the crew can leave it "parked" on the sea bed while they carry out their mission.

The SEALs use the Mark 8 Swimmer Delivery Vehicle (SDV), which can carry six soldiers. It is 30 feet (9 m) long and three feet (90 cm) wide. It has a shape like a **torpedo**. Powered by electric motors, the SDV can maintain an underwater speed of three to four knots (5.5–7.5 km) for several hours. However, the soldiers sit astride the SDV in their wet suits and their breathing equipment in a crouched posture that is very tiring physically. This means they have to rest onshore for several hours after their journey in order to recuperate.

Boats and **dinghies** offer a quicker way of getting elite forces teams onto a shore or riverbank. However, there are dangers involved with small boats. They have little protection and, if spotted, can be blown out of the water with relative ease. Outboard motors are noisy, but if the team decides to use oars or

For amphibious landings, this Zodiac speedboat is used to carry SEALs toward the enemy coastline. It is camouflaged in gray and black to avoid detection by coastal defenses and enemy aircraft.

paddles, it will take much longer to get to their destination. Nevertheless, small boats do have several advantages when it comes to inserting teams: they can transport large quantities of weapons and equipment and provide access to areas that are impenetrable to foot patrols, such as dense jungle.

Typical boats used by elite teams for infiltration include the British Rigid Raider, a small, fast craft used by British units such as the SAS, SBS (Special Boat Services), and Royal Marines for

Elite forces may infiltrate land positions using the enemy's vehicles—such as the armored High-Mobility Multi-purpose Wheeled Vehicle (HMMWV).

Colombian Marines rush ashore from their LVTP-7 landing vehicle on an amphibious operation. They are armed with M14 rifles.

amphibious operations. It is capable of carrying up to nine fully equipped troops at speeds up to 40 **knots** (76 km/hr). Then there is a range of inflatable boats, which are powered by outboard motors, and can carry up to 12 soldiers. On a river mission, two or more boats work as a team. One boat stops and its crew keep watch on the river ahead. The second boat, covered by the team on the bank, then moves forward to establish an observation position on the opposite bank. This process continues until the troops reach their destination.

Different vehicles are needed for infiltration on land. During World War II, for example, British SAS units used Willys Jeeps and a range of trucks to transport teams to and from targets in North Africa. This tradition was continued in the deserts of Iraq during the 1991 Gulf War, when SAS troops on heavily armed Land Rover 110 vehicles roamed behind enemy lines hunting for mobile Scud missile launchers. The Land Rovers were armed with a combination of heavy machine guns, Mark 19 grenade launchers, Milan antitank missiles, and Stinger surface-to-air missiles.

The Australian SAS also prefers Land Rover vehicles, which are ideal for coping with the long distances involved in operations in the vastness of the Australian outback. Units such as the U.S. Special Forces and Navy SEALs use the High Mobility Multi-Purpose Wheeled Vehicle (HMMWV), which is designed to operate in all types of terrain and weather conditions. More powerful vehicles are employed by the cavalry regiments of the French Foreign Legion. These include the AMX-10RC tank destroyer, which can knock out tanks with its 105-mm main gun. Whatever vehicles are being used, elite teams favor the hours of darkness for vehicle travel. This reduces the chances of convoys being spotted, especially by enemy aircraft.

Insertion over land using vehicles is not the only way elite teams can infiltrate enemy territory. Simply walking across borders is another means, though of course highly defended borders offer major obstacles. Modern borders can be guarded by many sophisticated defenses, such as **night-vision cameras** and invisible microwave beams, which trigger alarms. Watchtowers manned by guards, as well as barbed wired and ditches filled with anti-personnel mines (designed to inflict damage against people) can be found beyond these electronic defenses. Even darkness offers little cover, since the enemy can employ **image intensifiers** and **thermal imagers**. Because of these defenses, elite forces teams favor aerial or waterborne insertion as a way of getting into hostile territory.

HUMAN TORPEDOES

During World War II, British commandos used what were known as "human torpedoes" to sneak into German harbors and destroy and damage ships. These were boats that were shaped like torpedoes, but had seating on them for commando divers. The commandos would steer these boats under the hulls of German ships. Then the front of the boat, which contained explosives, was detached and left under the German boat to explode when the commandos were at a safe distance.

NIGHT OPERATIONS

Many Special Forces operations take place at night. By moving during hours of darkness, soldiers are able to stay hidden from the enemy, but it also means they must have all the essential skills of night fighting and navigation.

The night is the friend of Special Forces units. It lets teams infiltrate and move unseen through and across enemy lines, and it provides cover for a rapid withdrawal. But operating in darkness requires special training and preparation. Night-fighting puts unique strains on the human body.

The first problem that must be overcome at night is simply that the soldiers cannot see as well as in daylight. Human beings have a certain amount of night vision thanks to special cells in the eyes called rods. However, these rods need at least 30 minutes to get used to darkness and start to work properly. In addition, harsh sunlight will make seeing at night difficult for around 36 hours. That is why elite troops operating in high sunlight conditions, such as in the desert, will wear sunglasses during the day if operating at night.

At night, the eyes also have problems estimating distance. Small objects, for example, seem farther away and larger objects closer. However, hearing becomes more acute at night because of lower background noise, and cold, moist air carries sound better. Using

Night-vision goggles enhance the soldier's vision by about 50 times. They were used by the Special Forces during the Gulf War in 1991.

The 82nd Airborne Division jump from a C-141B Starlifter during a night exercise. During the Grenada conflict of 1983, this division worked with the First Ranger Battalion during Operation Urgent Fury.

hearing at night requires much training so the soldier can work out what the sounds are and where they are coming from. A rifle bolt being loaded, for example, can be heard from a great distance.

The sense of smell can also be used at night. Elite troops train themselves to face at an angle into the wind, relax, and breathe normally but take sharp, frequent sniffs. In this way, the soldier can pick up different smells, which may give clues as to the presence of an enemy. Elite teams operating at night need to take account of the problem of fatigue. Every team member should be allowed to get some rest, and there should be regular breaks for food and water. Very tired soldiers are a problem at night, since they do not think clearly. Commanders therefore must try to ensure the troops get some rest and food.

Silent movement at night is essential for Special Forces missions. Training emphasizes moving slowly with small, high steps, feeling carefully before shifting the weight onto the leading foot, while at the same time scanning ahead. Troops moving in single file must try to step in the footsteps of the soldier in front of them. Those spaces will have already been cleared of obstacles. This tactic will not only help silent movement, it will also deceive the enemy as to

When walking at night, lift the leg clear of the ground, then lower it slowly, feeling with the toe for any obstacles hidden in the darkness.

the size of the unit. All branches and bushes should be carefully pushed aside when moving and then replaced. If they are broken, they will leave white spots on the sides of trees or shrubs—these are very visible at night.

When moving at night, soldiers slowly lift their left legs to nearly knee height, balancing on the right, and then easing forward, while at the same time feeling for trip wires and twigs. The toe is pointed down and used to feel the ground with the outside of the toe of the boot. If all is clear, the toe is settled on the ground, then the heel, all the time feeling for loose rocks or twigs. When they are confident of a solid footing, soldiers slowly roll their weight forward and then, following a slight pause, begin to lift the right boot.

The view through night-vision goggles. The figures in the shot indicate enemy targets, who are unaware of the soldier's presence.

Nova goggles use a single image intensifier to help this British elite soldier see in the dark during a night exercise in Dartmoor, England.

Another tactic used at night when moving is stalking, or "the stalk." This is done when approaching a sentry, for example. The stalk is essentially walking at night, very slowly, in a crouch. Often the stalk is done by crawling, since a crawling soldier is very difficult for the enemy to see. The fastest crawl is made by pressing the arm and foot on the same side of the body against the ground to pull or push forward. This method can be rather noisy; a quieter way involves pressing down an arm and a foot on opposite sides and resting on one hip. An even quieter method of crawling involves using the toes and elbows to lift and move the torso forward slowly. When crawling, the soldier feels for twigs and rocks and either removes them or goes around them.

Night-fighting requires a great deal of training and practice, especially with regard to shooting. Precisely identifying targets at night may be difficult. A commander may put reflective or luminous marks on trees or rocks at certain places to tell the soldiers where their comrades are and who are the enemy. The height of the spots will be known to each member of the team, which will help aiming. Each member of the team will have also memorized the area in front of them so they can picture it at night. (The luminous dots will help them keep track of where features are.) If an enemy approach is heard, each soldier will be able to fire directly at targets even without seeing them. If footsteps are heard in dry bushes, for example, a soldier will be able to picture the area and know where they lie in relation to his position.

When it comes to actual night-fighting, some weapons are more effective than others. Rifles and machine guns equipped with night

"Dark room" training tests a soldier's reaction time. With dummies positioned behind him, he must assess their location, then shoot.

vision devices, for example, enable shooters to spot their targets. Image-intensifying sights are an excellent way of seeing in the dark. These sights operate by amplifying low levels of visible light up to 100,000 times to let the soldier see even on the darkest night. Because of their light weight, image intensifiers are often mounted on rifles and machine guns, as well as being carried in the hand. They are also undetectable by an adversary. However, they are not as effective in smoke, dense foliage, fog, and heavy rain or snow. A more sophisticated device is the thermal imager (TI), which operates rather like a television camera but creates a picture using infrared "heat" differences instead of light. A TI system can see men or machines through smoke, foliage, or **camouflage**, by day or by night.

By using technology and moving **stealthily**, the elite soldiers will be able to fight and move at night with all the confidence they would have in the daytime.

SEEING AT NIGHT

When looking at an object in darkness, elite soldiers train themselves to look at the edge of the object rather than straight on. This is because the human eye sees better at an angle in conditions of darkness. Try this experiment: In a dark room, look at a closed door with a light behind it. If you stare into the center of the door, its outline will start to disappear. If you look at its outline, you can still make out its shape. The elite forces apply this when looking at enemy soldiers at night.

AMBUSHES

The ambush is without doubt one of the most effective weapons in the Special Forces armory when behind enemy lines. However, ambushes need expert planning if they are to work at their best.

Put simply, an ambush is a surprise attack on an enemy formation with the intention of destroying it. The key to an ambush is shock action—a quick attack followed by a speedy withdrawal. The action should be over within two minutes maximum, although elite units often finish the job in less than 30 seconds.

An elite ambushing unit is made up of three parts: the support element, the assault element, and the security element. The support element is usually made up of the commander, radio operators, and medics. The assault element has the task of destroying the enemy in the actual ambush. The security element does just that—provides security. It watches out for any enemy reinforcements and also helps their comrades to escape after the attack. In many ways, the security element is one of the most important parts of the operation. Security around the ambush site itself must be tight at all times until the moment when the ambush is sprung.

When planning for an ambush, troops need a lot of information about the enemy. Planning involves working out what

All five brigades of the Italian Alpini (Italy's mountain troops) are experts in winter warfare. This soldier is armed with a Beretta BM59.

type of ambush is required for the task. For example, an ambush against enemy tanks needs antitank weapons and explosives. Timing is one of the most important aspects of the ambush. An ambush sprung in darkness, for example, will achieve more surprise and confusion than one sprung in daylight. The ambushers need to study the ambush site, being careful not to give the enemy any clues that an ambush is going to take place. In addition to this, the elite forces commander will find out all about the enemy that is to be ambushed, including the number of

Armed with M16s, soldiers from the Special Forces were always on alert for ambush as they patrolled Saigon, South Vietnam, 1969.

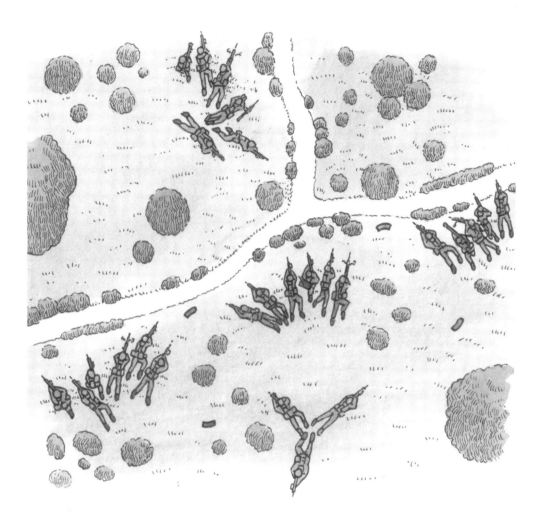

This ambush formation has a central group acting as a command center, with the outlying groups offering protective or attacking support as needed. Each group must hold its individual position, otherwise all the others are put at risk.

soldiers, their weapons, and where they will be. Once he or she has this information, the ambush commander will select the ambush site itself and put the soldiers in place, ready and waiting. When the enemy arrives, then they can spring the ambush and open fire.

Snipers must be excellent shots and have the patience to lie still for hours waiting for their enemy targets.

One very important quality for elite soldiers to have is patience. Once an ambush is set, the soldiers might have to wait for many days until their target arrives. Soldiers who get fidgety and bored will let their attention wander, and they might miss the signs that the enemy is approaching them.

The majority of Special Forces' work involves watching and waiting for the action to start. That is why, during recruitment, elite regiments test a candidate's ability to wait around without complaining. In the British Parachute Regiment, recruits are made to sit on a cold hill facing a wall for many hours. The trainers watch them to see who cannot cope with the inactivity. Those that cannot fail the course because they will not make good elite soldiers .

Once an ambush is over, the commander needs to get the troops out quickly. The noise made by the ambush may have alerted other enemy forces, or reinforcements may already be on their way. The commander will evacuate the ambush site quickly. This is done in stages, with the assault element pulling out first and the security element covering. When pulling out, the idea is to create maximum deception as the various elements withdraw to their rallying points. If the enemy is pursuing, the security element will use fire and movement to slow them down. In the case of a pursuit, the various elements of the ambush party may split into small groups to evade the pursuers.

This British soldier uses prismatic binoculars (designed to break up beams of light) to survey an enemy base. He is prepared with rations and nighttime equipment for a long exercise.

Elite units operating behind enemy lines must also know what to do if they themselves are ambushed. The key to a successful counterambush is hitting back immediately. Firing right back gives the ambushed team time to escape and confuses the enemy. This helps to boost the unit's morale: a unit that survives an ambush and mounts a successful **counterattack** is going to feel better about itself, and the enemy will feel worse. At the least, counter-ambush tactics give time for reinforcements to arrive. But what are counterambush tactics?

The most important thing is to keep moving when fired on, either charging the ambushers or running around them and then mounting a counterattack from the flanks. All available firepower should be brought to bear on the ambushers, including

SPOTTING AN AMBUSH

The following signs can tell an elite unit that there is an ambush waiting for them:

- Birds fly suddenly out of the trees as if startled.
- Plants growing by the side of the road or track have been disturbed.
- Human footprints can be seen on the ground around them.
- Metal can be seen glinting in the foliage.
- Buildings appear deserted—they may have been cleared out for use in the ambush.

automatic fire, explosives, grenades, and even antitank rockets when available.

However, care must be taken not to fall into a trap. The ambushers might have actually set up two ambushes: one for an initial attack and another to attack the counterattack!

Elite forces units, however, usually see any traps before they actually happen. This is because they are experts in tracking enemy movements and spotting hidden enemy soldiers. We will look at the skills that they need to be able to do this in the next chapter.

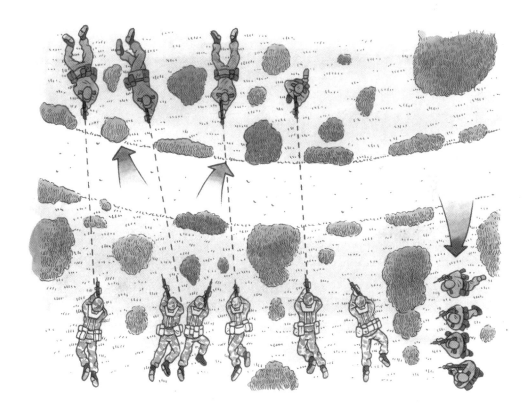

An ambush cannot be anticipated, but the effect can be minimized. Here, the ambushed party (top) make optimum use of a rearguard (right) to perform a flanking retaliation on the enemy (center).

TRACKING AND MOVING

Elite soldiers behind enemy lines might be fighting an enemy who is also in hiding. That is why it is essential that they know how to move safely and silently and also how to track the enemy's movements.

It is vital that an elite soldier knows where he or she is at all times behind enemy lines. If soldiers get lost, then they are more likely to be discovered and their mission is more likely to fail. An important aspect of navigation is called "**Terrain Analysis.**" This means looking at the ground in front of you, then looking at the map, and seeing if there are any differences between the two. Terrain analysis involves things like working out which way the rivers run, which features can be seen at night, and the positioning of fences and other man-made features. In terrain such as dense jungle, where the only thing to be seen is trees, elite soldiers will have to use their compasses to navigate, which will mean literally holding it in front of them. At night, the military compasses are luminous (they glow in the dark) so that they can still be seen.

Another method of navigating is called "**dead reckoning.**" Dead reckoning means that soldiers plot their journey before they set out on a mission, and plan it in a series of stages. Each one is measured in terms of distance and direction between two points.

A standard-issue compass and map is essential for navigation. Maps must have plastic coverings to protect them from water damage.

Makeshift maps may be drawn on the ground when briefing in the field, as used in this National Guard exercise.

These courses lead them from the starting point to the final destination. They help the soldiers to find out where they are at any one time, either by following their plan or by comparing where they are on the ground to where they are on the map.

Once they have worked out where they are going and plotted their route on a map, elite soldiers will mark out **route cards**. This describes each stage of the route they intend to travel. When they have completed their route cards, they are ready to move. When moving, they must keep a careful record of the direction they are heading in and the distance they have covered. If they deviate from their route, they must make adjustments to the route cards and map-reading. However, if they are operating in an area where contact with the enemy is likely, they will not write anything down, because this information may be useful to an enemy if they are captured.

Knowing as much as possible about the enemy will help an elite team find out valuable military information. This involves knowing where the enemy is and what he is doing, and this must be done by tracking. A careless enemy will leave telltale signs of his presence, which can then be used against him. Moved stones, crumbled stones pressed into the earth, or bent grasses are signs that an enemy patrol has been in the area. Stains are another sign. These may include blood, water on stones, and crushed leaves.

Garbage is an example of the presence of ill-disciplined soldiers, though booby traps may have been left among the garbage to kill the unwary. Sounds can also tell the elite unit where the enemy is. Soldiers can place their ears on the ground or on a stick driven six inches (15 cm) into the ground. It is hard to work out the direction of the noises, but sounds can be heard from a

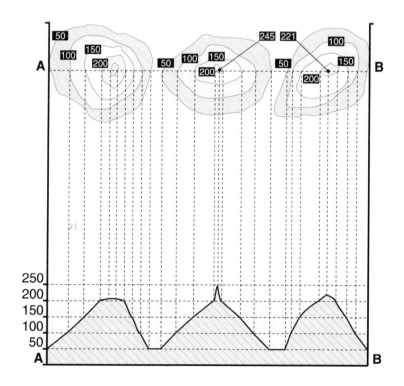

Contour lines on a map indicate to soldiers the height of the ground in which they are operating and the steepness of the slopes.

Elite soldiers must "read the ground" for signs of enemy presence, such as footprints, garbage, and evidence of fire and shelter.

long distance because the ground actually carries noise better than the air. In addition, sounds will carry farther in light mist, though they can be masked by rain or wind. Rain may also cause soldiers to miss sounds if they are wearing hoods or caps—it is often worth having a wet head in order to hear telltale sounds. During a night operation, no one should wear a hat or a helmet. Helmets make hollow sounds in the rain, whistle during breezes, and generally rattle and rustle. These noises mean that important sounds may be missed.

Poor enemy camouflage can also be a signpost to an attacking team. In particular, team members should look for straight lines (rarely found in nature), unusual differences in color or tone, and unnatural vegetation, such as green leaves among dead branches. Having detected the enemy, a team must work out their distance to them. This is not easy. Judging distances depends on a soldier's skill and the amount of water vapor in the air. Clear, dry desert air, for example, helps a soldier to detect sights at a greater distance, but does not carry sound or odors as well as more **humid** air. Sounds can be a real problem when estimating distances, since they can bounce among buildings and rocky terrain and mislead an individual as to the direction of their source. Sound travels at around 1,000 feet (300 m) per second, so the elite soldier should count the seconds between seeing the flash of a weapon firing and hearing its bang. The number of seconds multiplied by three equates to the distance to the weapon in hundreds of meters.

Even if elite soldiers are master shots with their rifles, or experts at blowing up bridges, they must still learn how to become virtually invisible while doing all these things. This, in short, is the art of hiding.

British Marines from the Mountain and Arctic Warfare Cadre test navigation equipment during training exercises in Norway, 2000.

AVOIDING THE ENEMY

Elite soldiers behind enemy lines cannot do anything very useful if they have been detected. The three essential techniques of remaining unseen are known as cover, concealment, and camouflage.

Concealment is the art of stopping yourself from being seen. It may be natural concealment—such as bushes, grass, and shadows—or artificial, with the soldier using materials such as camouflage nets. Successful concealment, both natural and artificial, may depend on the season, weather, and light.

Camouflage is what the soldiers use to mask the color, outline, or texture of themselves and their equipment. Vegetation or other materials that grow in the area provide natural, and the best, camouflage. When looked at closely, man-made substances will always appear to be man-made. The secret of camouflage is to never draw the attention of the enemy or create a reason for the enemy to investigate your position.

There are many things that can give you away. These include cut branches when you are building a concealed shelter (known as a "**hide**"); poorly concealed hide edges; equipment left outside the hide; and, of course, garbage left outside the hide. A soldier needs to remember that the enemy can smell, too: food should be eaten without cooking if possible. The enemy also has ears. Moving as soundlessly as possible is essential.

The ghillie suit, as worn by these U.S. Rangers, is made from strips of camouflage cloth, and is ideal for operations in deciduous forests.

Anything that might rattle should be taped down to keep it quiet. Messages between team members should be given by hand signal. Sound carries best at night, so at this time noise of any kind has to be reduced to zero.

When communicating, do not imitate birdcalls. Unless your enemy is stupid, they will know your signals are not birds chirping. Most birds call in the early morning and evening. They do not call to each other in the middle of the night. Owls hoot, but how many owls do you hear? Are they native to the area? Owls stick to one area their entire lives. If the enemy has been in an area for several weeks without hearing an owl, and then they hear two of them hooting back and forth, they are not going to think it is two owls. Any noise you make will be assumed a threat and the enemy will fire.

Desert camouflage uses brown and sandy tones as disguise.

When it comes to what the enemy might see, the standard fieldcraft drill is to remember the "Five Ss": Shape, Shine, Shadow, Silhouette, and Spacing.

This means that straight lines—a sure sign of a human presence—should be avoided. Cover rifle barrels with bits of camouflaged material. Anything reflective or bright should be made dull, from the human face (camouflaged with greasepaint) to the heels of boots. Anything smooth should be made rough or crinkly. Movement should be within shadows wherever possible, and creating shadows, even on the body, should be avoided. Keep away from crests and skylines because you will stand out in silhouette.

Soldiers have to be prepared to move slowly to their objective. The enemy—for trainee soldiers, that is the instructors—will notice not only human movement, but sudden flights (and the alarm calls) of birds or animals, odd movements of plants and bushes, and so on. Camouflage has to be the right color, and may have to be changed frequently so that the soldier constantly blends into the background. Grass and saplings grow up toward the sun: a patch of strangely flattened vegetation will instantly raise suspicion and if—even more remarkably—it is seen to move, it will draw fire.

The soldier's best hope of remaining invisible when moving in grass and woodland is the "**ghillie suit**." A ghillie suit is an outfit made up of hundreds of strips of camouflaged cloth. The soldier ends up looking like a bedraggled scarecrow, but the camouflage is excellent. The suit, which can take up to 50 hours to make, was first created by gamekeepers (ghillies) in the Scottish Highlands in the 19th century.

Camouflage cream blacks out the entire face, as used by this U.S. Marine during operational training.

A ghillie suit is hot and heavy. But surviving on the modern battlefield has never been too elegant a matter.

In cities, various shades of gray seem to make the most effective camouflage, and here the occasional straight line and smooth surface will blend into the man-made background. White suits, usually looser than standard uniform to break up the human profile, are worn against full snow or ice, but where there is ground snow but none on the trees, a woodland camouflage jacket and white trousers is the best outfit to choose. In desert country, a ghillie suit is usually no use—not much can be done to blur a person's shape against sand. Using sand-colored uniforms in the camouflage suit pattern, and whatever local vegetation there is (if any), are the soldier's best hopes.

When on a **reconnaissance** mission, one of the best ways to stay hidden is by building a camouflaged shelter (a "hide"). What kind of hide the soldier builds, depends on the mission. It may be a quick hide, simply an arrangement of bushes and grasses to conceal the soldier for only a few minutes. A long **surveillance** mission, on the other hand, can involve building a complex shelter (a job most safely done at night) with a roof and observation holes through which to view the enemy. The front of such a hide should be made **bulletproof**, often by heaping up a bank of soil and turf in front of it. The hide should be big enough to give the team some movement to enable them to exercise stiff muscles. Perhaps most important, the hide should not be set up in a position that is altogether obviously "ideal" for reconnaissance, like the tops of hills. The enemy will no doubt have checked out all such positions and will be watching them.

If soldiers follow all these techniques, then they should be able to operate behind enemy lines without being discovered. It takes nerves of steel to survive surrounded by the enemy, but the world's elite forces are trained to do just that.

HIDING FOR LONG PERIODS

If elite soldiers need to hide silently in one place for a long time, they will do well to obey the following rules:

- Every hour or so, stretch out each leg so that limbs do not go "dead." This means that they will be able to move quickly if they have to escape.
- Be sure to eat and drink to keep their energy levels up, but do not leave any garbage that could tell the enemy they are there.
- Do mental tasks. Otherwise they may become bored and miss important events in front of them.

GLOSSARY

Barometric trigger A special device that opens a parachute automatically when a parachutist reaches a certain height.

Booby traps Explosive devices, hidden in harmless-looking objects. They explode unexpectedly when enemy soldiers get close.

Bulletproof Something is bulletproof when bullets cannot go through it. Soldiers often wear bulletproof jackets to protect themselves in battle.

Civilian Irregular Defense Groups (CIDGs) Special groups of civilian soldiers created by U.S. Special Forces during the Vietnam War.

Counterattack An attack made by a group of soldiers in response to an attack by the enemy.

Counterinsurgency A type of war fought against guerrilla soldiers or an undercover enemy.

Dead reckoning A way of navigating by plotting your journey from one point to the next and so on until your reach your destination.

Dinghies Inflatable rubber life rafts.

Drop Zone (DZ) The first place where soldiers are deployed on a mission.

Ghillie suit A special camouflaged suit made out of strips of material.

Guerrilla A civilian soldier who fights against a country's official government or army.

HAHO High-Altitude High-Opening—a type of parachute technique.

HALO High-Altitude Low-Opening—a type of parachute technique.

Hide A camouflaged shelter.

Humid Having lots of water vapor in the air.

Image intensifiers Special sights that magnify light and help soldiers to see in the dark.

Infiltration To enter a forbidden or dangerous place secretly without being noticed. Used by the world's Special Forces.

Limpet mines Explosive magnetic devices that can be stuck to metal objects and set to explode.

Knot A measurement of speed equal to one nautical mile (6,076 feet/ 1,852 m) per hour.

Night-vision cameras Cameras that let soldiers see in the dark.

Reconnaissance Watching the enemy to gain information that you can use to defeat him.

Rendezvous point A place where everyone meets.

Route card A piece of card on which soldiers mark their journey route.

Scuba Portable tanks full of air that divers strap to their backs for breathing underwater. The word comes from Self-contained Underwater Breathing Apparatus.

Static-line drops A type of parachute jump in which a long wire attached to the plane pulls the parachute from the pack so that it opens.

Stealthily Moving carefully and quietly so as not to be detected.

Surveillance Watching something closely.

Terrain Analysis Studying the ground to work out how to cross it.

Thermal imagers Devices which can "see" heat and let soldiers operate at night.

Torpedo A long tubular weapon fired underwater and used to sink ships.

Tracking The process of finding and following an enemy.

INTERNATIONAL TRAVEL ADVICE

Africa

Angola—The northeast of the country is out of bounds to foreigners.

Botswana—Stay away from government soldiers, who might arrest you.

Congo—Do not talk about politics; this issue can land you in prison.

Gabon—Have your papers with you at all times, because the police like to pick on foreign visitors.

Kenya—Watch out for thieves, especially in the capital Nairobi.

Libya—Do not photograph any government buildings.

Sudan—Do not bring expensive items into the country; they will usually be stolen.

Middle East

Kuwait—Do not travel in the desert; there are lots of mines there left over from the Gulf War.

Saudi Arabia—Be especially respectful of women and religious buildings.

Asia

Cambodia—Lots of bombs and weapons litter the countryside left behind after wars there. Do not touch them.

China—Many thieves prey on tourists, so keep a close guard at all times.

India—Theft and robbery is a big problem in India.

Pakistan—Women should wear modest clothes that cover their bodies.

Thailand—Saying anything bad about the Thai royal family could put you in jail.

Vietnam—Unexploded bombs litter the Vietnamese countryside, so don't wander off paths.

Central and South America

Bolivia—Avoid the Chapare region. Illegal drugs are grown here and if you wander off the highway, you could be shot.

Brazil—Do not carry anything that looks expensive because violent theft is very common, especially in the cities.

Columbia—Three U.S. citizens were kidnapped and killed in 1999. There is widespread guerilla and paramilitary activity across the country. There have been cases of mass kidnappings from churches and restaurants, but foreigners were not specifically targeted in these instances.

Europe

Armenia, Azerbaijan, and Georgia—Be very careful if visiting these countries, because there is often fighting between rival ethnic groups.

Chechyna—Kidnapping, war, and the murder of foreigners makes this country very dangerous.

The former Yugoslavia—Yugoslavia has now split into separate countries following a civil war. The Federal Republic of Yugoslavia (FRY) is made up of two republics, Serbia and Montenegro; the region of Kosovo has been under U.N. administrative control since June 1999. Get tourist center advice before you travel to any of these countries, avoid visiting Kosovo unless absolutely essential, avoid speaking Serbian or discussing the political situation, and do not touch any weapons you might find.

USEFUL WEBSITES

http://www.snipercountry.com/survival.htm
http://www.vulcan.belvoir.army.mil
http://clevermedia.com/arcade/ambush.html
http://www.etravel.com
http://www.state.gov/other

http://www.travel.roughguides.com
http://www.ease.com
http://www.tips4travel.com
http://www.eurotrip.com

FURTHER READING

Beckett, Ian. *Encyclopedia of Guerrilla Warfare*. Oxford, England: ABC Clio, 2000

Breuer, William B. *Daring Missions of World War II*. New York: John Wiley and Sons, 2001.

Carss, Bob. *The Complete Guide to Tracking*. London: Constable, 1999.

Hunt, Ray C. and Bernard Norling. *Behind Japanese Lines: An American Guerrilla in the Philippines*. Lexington: University Press of Kentucky, 2000.

McNab, Andy. *Bravo Two Zero*. London: Corgi, 1994.

Scott-Donelan. *Tactical Tracking Operations*. Boulder, Colo.: Paladin Press, 1998.

Stafford, David. *Secret Agent: The True Story of the Special Operations Executive*. London: BBC Consumer Publishing, 2000.

Thompson, Julian. *The Imperial War Museum's Book of War Behind Enemy Lines*. London: Pan, 1999.

Walker, Greg. *At the Hurricane's Eye—US Special Forces from Vietnam to Desert Storm*. New York: Ivy Books, 1994.

White, Terry. *Fighting Skills of the SAS and Special Forces*. London: Constable Robinson, 1997.

ABOUT THE AUTHOR

Dr. Chris McNab has written and edited numerous books on military history and elite forces survival. His publications to date include *German Paratroopers of World War II*, *The Illustrated History of the Vietnam War*, *First Aid Survival Manual*, and *Special Forces Endurance Techniques*, as well as many articles and features in other works. Forthcoming publications include books on the SAS, while Chris's wider research interests lie in literature and ancient history. Chris lives in South Wales, U.K.

INDEX

References in italics refer to illustrations